Find Out About It!

By Gill Stacey

CELEBRATION PRESS
Pearson Learning Group

Contents

Writing a Research Report 3
Step 1: Plan Your Work 4
Step 2: Choose a Topic 6
Step 3: Find Information 8
Step 4: Make an Outline 16
Step 5: Write Your Report 18
Step 6: Present Your Report 22
Glossary 23
Index 24

Writing a Research Report

Your teacher has just told you to write a research report. Now what do you do? Don't worry. Doing research and writing a report can be fun. You could even become an expert on your topic.

A research report presents information on a particular topic. The writer gathers information from sources such as books, **encyclopedias**, magazines, newspapers, and the Internet. Through step-by-step instructions, this book shows you how to plan your work, find and organize information, and write and present your report.

I'm Oscar Owl. I'll help you at each step of writing your report!

STEP 1 Plan Your Work

Before you begin your assignment, review the information from your teacher to see how long the report should be and when it is due. For example, you might have about three weeks to write a history report. It's a good idea to make a work planner to keep you on schedule.

Materials
- ✔ a pencil
- ✔ a calendar
- ✔ a notebook or writing paper
- ✔ notecards
- ✔ sticky notes
- ✔ a library card
- ✔ a highlighter

How to Plan Your Work

1 List each step in writing your research report. The steps are on the planner on page 5.

2 Divide up the time that you have for the whole project and give yourself a date, or deadline, to finish each step. Finding information will probably take the most time.

3 Write your deadlines on the planner.

4 Check your planner every day to make sure that you're on schedule.

My Research Report Work Planner

Day		Step	Done
Thu	1	Choose a topic.	☐
Fri	2	Find information. Take notes.	☐
Sat	3		☐
Sun	4		☐
Mon	5		☐
Tue	6		☐
Wed	7		☐
Thu	8	Organize notes. Make an outline.	☐
Fri	9		☐
Sat	10		☐
Sun	11		☐
Mon	12	Write the report.	☐
Tue	13		☐
Wed	14		☐
Thu	15		☐
Fri	16	Practice presenting the report.	☐
Sat	17		☐
Sun	18		☐
Mon	19	Present the report!	☐

STEP 2

Choose a Topic

You have been assigned to write a report on the history of transportation. The history of transportation is a large topic. It covers hundreds of years and there are many kinds of transportation, such as cars, boats, planes, and trains. Researching a topic like this could take years, so you will need to narrow it down.

How to Choose a Topic

1 Write down as many ideas that you can think of about the topic. This is called brainstorming.

2 Now narrow down your list. Cross off topics that are too general for one report or too narrow. Cross off any ideas that don't interest you or are not related to your topic.

3 Circle the topic that you would like to know more about.

History of Transportation: Topic Ideas

~~The history of ships and boats~~
Too broad – it would take me a year to write all that.

~~How to sail a boat~~
I'd like to know this, but it doesn't fit the assignment.

(The Titanic)

The Titanic was a famous ship that sank. Why did it sink? I'd like to know more about it.

④ Think about what you want to know about your topic and ask questions to help you gather the facts. Use words such as *who*, *what*, *when*, *where*, *why*, and *how* to form your questions.

⑤ Write your questions on a sheet of paper. Use your questions as a checklist while you research to be sure you cover all the important facts.

The *Titanic*

The sinking of the *Titanic* was one of the world's most famous transportation disasters. The *Titanic* was sailing from Southampton, England, to New York City, United States, when it hit an iceberg. The accident happened on April 14, 1912.

Titanic Questions

What was the Titanic?

How was the Titanic different from other ships?

Who was on the ship? Who built it?

When did it sink?

Why did it sink?

What did people learn from the disaster?

Why do we still remember it today?

newspaper reports and photos from the time

STEP 3 Find Information

Now it's time to find out more about your topic. Remember, an interesting report presents information from several sources. You can look for information in books, in magazines, in newspapers, in encyclopedias, on the Internet, and by watching educational programs on television.

Use an Encyclopedia

Encyclopedia articles give basic facts, so they are a good place to start your research. Most encyclopedias have a series of books or volumes. Topics are listed in alphabetical order.

How to Use an Encyclopedia

1. Make a list of keywords related to your topic.

2. Look for your keywords in the correct volume of the encyclopedia. Each volume will have a number or range of letters on its spine to guide you.

3. Use the **guide words** at the top of each page to find your topic. Then use the **entry words** on the page to find the article.

Research Tip

Keywords are important words related to your topic. For example, you might use keywords such as *Titanic*, *ships*, and *shipwrecks* when researching the *Titanic*.

4 Check the list of related topics at the end of the article to see if they lead you to more information.

5 Most **reference books** cannot be taken out of a library. Use small sticky notes to mark the pages you want to take notes from later.

Encyclopedia Article

Ships

Titanic

guide word

entry word

On the morning of April 10, 1912, nearly 2,000 passengers boarded the *Titanic*, which was on its first sea voyage from Southampton, England, to New York. The ship could carry up to 3,547 passengers and crew. No expense was spared in making the *Titanic* and it was the grandest ship at that time. Everything on board was brand new or specially made for the ship; everything was designed to make the passengers comfortable and to entertain them during the voyage.

The *Titanic*'s builders claimed the ship was "virtually unsinkable" and most people believed there was no chance that the ship would sink. However, on April 14, 1912, the *Titanic* collided with an iceberg in the Atlantic Ocean. In less than three hours the ship sank. In total, 1,490 passengers died.

The *Titanic* was a floating hotel. First-class passengers paid a lot of money to travel in complete luxury.

Model of the *Titanic*

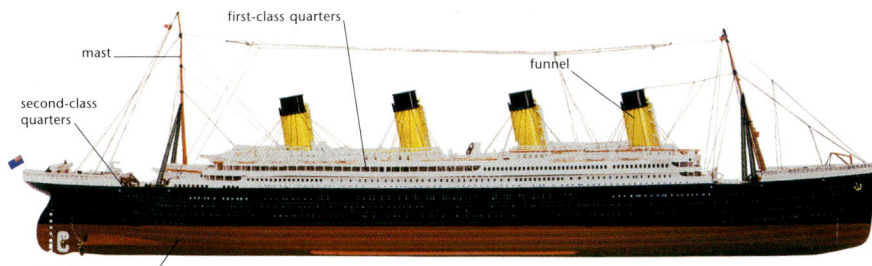

first-class quarters
mast
funnel
second-class quarters
third-class quarters

Iceberg
Icebergs are large pieces of ice that have detached from glaciers in the ocean. Icebergs drift slowly in the ocean and can be dangerous for ships.

Dinner plates found on the wreck.   restored plate

9

Use the Library

Most libraries have hundreds of books, so finding information on your topic might seem overwhelming. Fortunately, nonfiction books are organized by a system of numbers called the **Dewey Decimal System**. Each book has its own number that you can find in the **card catalog**. The card catalog lists books by the subject, author, and title.

Subject Card

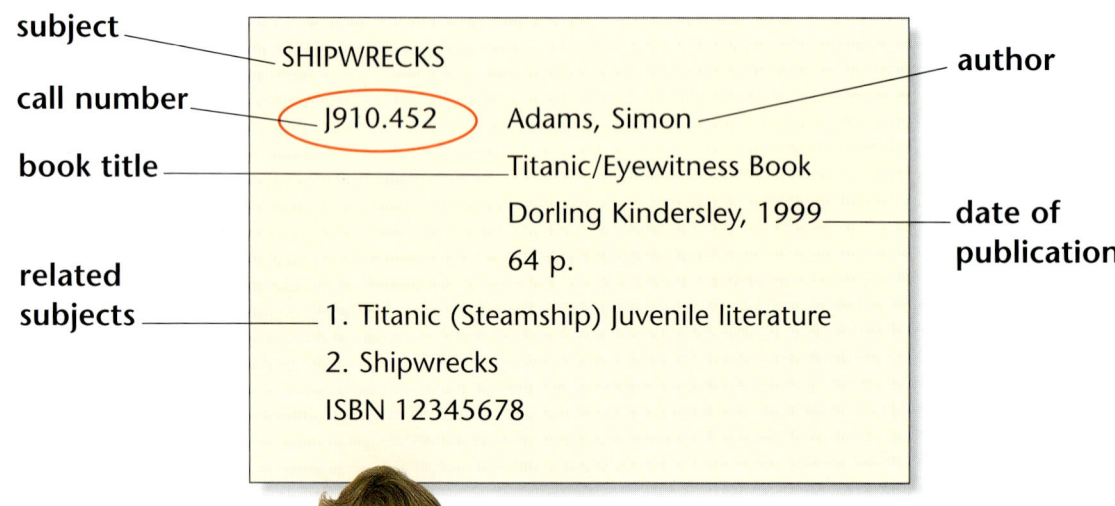

Research Tip

Some card catalogs are printed on index cards and some are on computers. They are organized in the same way. If you need help using the card catalog, ask a librarian.

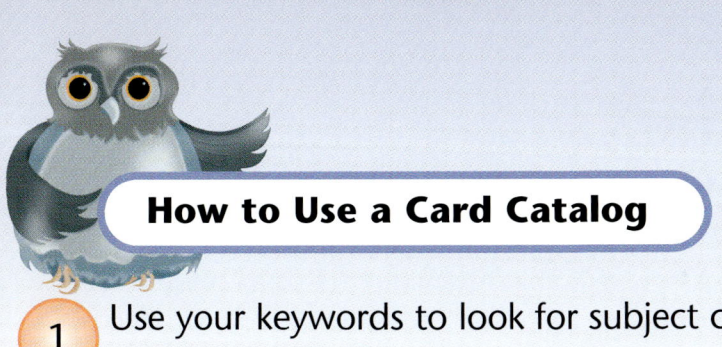

How to Use a Card Catalog

1. Use your keywords to look for subject cards in the card catalog. If you are using a computer catalog, select the subject search and enter one or two keywords.

2. Find the **call number** of the book. This number tells you the book's location. The letter J stands for **juvenile**, meaning it will be in the children's section.

3. Write down the call numbers and titles of the books you want to find.

4. Use the call number to locate each book on the shelves. Most libraries have signs on the shelves that will guide you with a range of numbers, such as 0–100. Locate the range that includes your call numbers and select your books.

5. Check out your books with your library card.

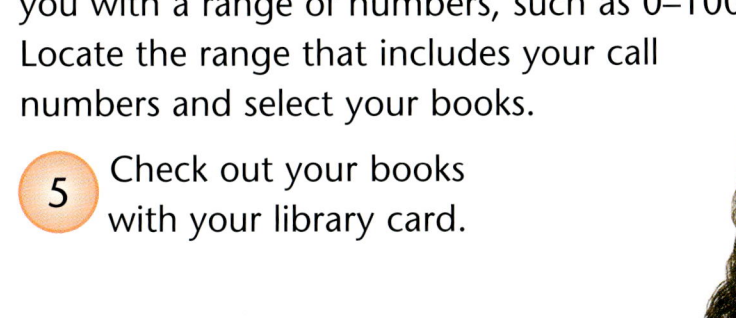

Search the Internet

Information for your report is at your fingertips. You just have to sit down at a computer and search the Internet. If you don't have a computer, ask the librarian to help you connect to the Internet in the library.

How to Search the Internet

1 Open the **browser** by clicking on it with your mouse.

2 Go to the box labeled *Address* on your browser and type in the name of a **search engine** to find Web sites related to your topic. Ask a librarian to suggest a good search engine.

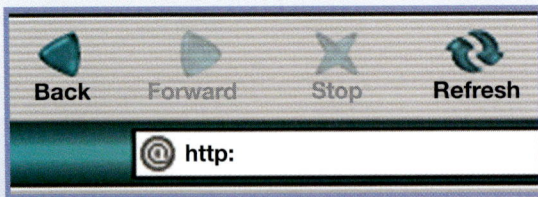

address box

3 Now type one or two of your keywords in the *Search* box and hit the *Enter* or *Return* button. A list of Web sites with brief descriptions will appear on your screen.

Research Tip
Not all Web sites have good information. Ask a librarian, a teacher, or another adult to suggest some reliable sites. Be sure that you have the correct spellings of the Web addresses.

④ Read the descriptions and click on a Web site that looks promising.

⑤ Scan the page to see if the article has information you need. Print out any useful pages and record the Web site addresses.

⑥ Click on the arrow or *Back* button to return to the search engine results so you can try other Web sites.

⑦ Read the pages you printed. Use a highlighter to mark the important information or take notes.

In 1912, most people got information about the *Titanic* by reading newspapers.

Today, many people get their information from the Internet.

13

Take Notes

Once you have found all of your information, it's time to take notes. Lined notecards or index cards are good for note-taking. Do not copy information word-for-word. Use your own words.

How to Take Notes

1. Write your research questions at the top of your notecards and then see how your sources answer the questions.

2. Write facts and details on the notecards to answer each question. You don't need to write in complete sentences.

3. Record where you found the information on each card. Include the title, author, publisher, and date of publication for books and articles. Write down the Web addresses and the authors of Web sites.

4. Keep taking notes until you have enough facts to write your report. You can have more than one notecard for each question.

How was the Titanic different from other ships?
- the largest ship of its time
- thought to be unsinkable
- had many elegant rooms and other features
- was one of the first ships to have gym and swimming pool

Sloan, Frank. <u>Titanic.</u> Austin: Raintree Steck-Vaughn, 1998.

The *Titanic* had a grand staircase.

Why did the Titanic sink?
- going too fast in the icy water
- hit an iceberg
- iceberg caused cracks and holes in the ship
- water flooded too many compartments in the bottom of the ship

World Book Encyclopedia, "Titanic". Chicago: World Book Inc., 2002.

The *Titanic* hit an iceberg similar to this one when in the North Atlantic Ocean.

STEP 4: Make an Outline

By now you probably have information from several different sources. You should organize your information before you begin writing. Follow these steps to prepare an outline of your report.

How to Make an Outline

1. Organize your notecards into groups of related questions. Each pile of cards represents a main idea.

2. Begin your outline with the **Roman numeral** I and label it *Introduction*.

3. Write each main idea beside another Roman numeral (II, III, and so on.) Leave plenty of space between each one.

4. Add details that support your main ideas. Label each detail by using capital letters *A, B,* or *C,* and so on. Use *1, 2,* and *3* to number any information that you add under the *A, B,* or *C* headings. (See page 17.)

5. Read your outline to see if the order of the information makes sense. Rearrange the sections if you need to.

6. Add one last Roman numeral and label it *Conclusion*.

title of paper — The Sinking of the Titanic

introduction labeled as "I" — I. Introduction
    A. What the Titanic was
    B. Why it is famous

main ideas: each main idea should have at least two details

II. Facts about the Titanic
    A. Why it was built
    B. What was special about it?
        1. People thought it was unsinkable
        2. Most luxurious ship built at that time
        3. Had many rich and famous passengers

III. What happened?
    A. Hit an iceberg
    B. Why it sank
    C. How people got off the ship
    D. Why so many died

IV. The wreck
    A. When it was found
    B. What we learned

last Roman numeral is "Conclusion" — V. Conclusion

A photo of the Titanic from 1912.

The bow of the Titanic has layers of rust from years of being under water.

About 700 passengers, mostly women and children, boarded lifeboats and were saved.

STEP 5: Write Your Report

You've organized your information, so you're finally ready to write. Use your notes and your outline to guide you while you write your report.

How to Write Your Report

1. Review your notecards and outline. Think about who will read your report.

2. Begin your report with an *Introduction* that tells your readers what your report is about and grabs their interest.

3. Write the main text of your report. Use your outline to write a paragraph for each main idea and use your notecards to fill in any missing details.

4. End your report with a *Conclusion*. Remind your readers what you think is most important about your topic.

title — **The Titanic**

introduction — The Titanic was one of the most famous ships that was ever built. People remember the Titanic because it sank on its first voyage. This disaster shocked the world.

main text — On April 14, 1912, crew members aboard the Titanic saw a huge iceberg. They tried to turn the ship, but the ship was too big and it was going too fast. The Titanic hit the iceberg. The iceberg cut holes in the ship's side and the ship began to fill with water. The crew knew that the ship would sink in a few hours.

conclusion — Everyone thought that the Titanic was unsinkable, so they were shocked when it sank. It was a sad lesson, but the Titanic disaster taught people how to travel more safely by ship. People will always remember the Titanic.

This activity is continued on page 20.

⑤ Revise your draft. Make sure that:
• the report is the right length
• the organization makes sense
• your questions are answered
• all the information relates to the topic.

⑥ Edit and polish your report by checking your spelling, capitalization, grammar, and punctuation so you can correct any mistakes.

Remember to check your spelling on the computer or in a dictionary.

Bibliography

Adams, Simon. <u>Eyewitness Guides: Titanic</u>. London: Dorling Kindersley, 1999.

Kamuda, Edward S. "Titanic: Past and Present." The Titanic Historical Society, Inc. http://www.titanic1org.articles

Sloan, Frank. <u>Titanic</u>. Austin: Raintree Steck-Vaughn, 1998.

"Titanic," <u>World Book Encyclopedia</u>. Chicago: World Book Inc., 2002.

7 List the sources that you used in alphabetical order on a separate sheet of paper. (Use the source information that you recorded while taking notes.) This is called a bibliography.

8 Create a cover and add illustrations. Number the pages and attach them together, with the bibliography as the last page.

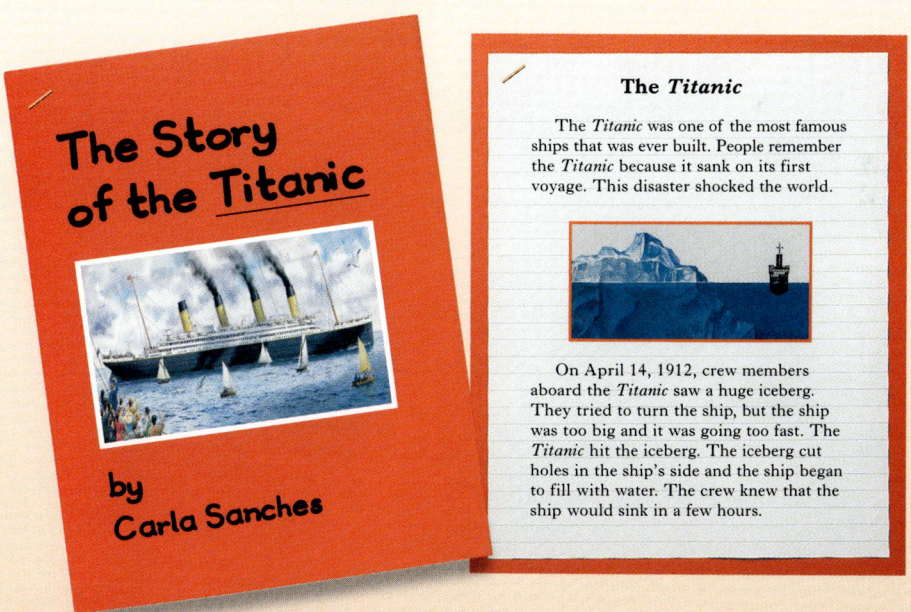

STEP 6: Present Your Report

If you followed the steps in this book, you've done a fine job writing your report. Now all you have left to do is present it to others. Practice your presentation with these steps and relax.

How to Prepare Your Presentation

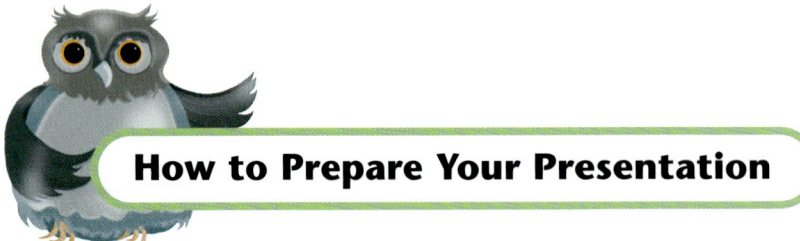

1. Read your report aloud or silently several times.

2. Underline or highlight the main ideas in your report so you can focus on the most important information.

3. Stand in front of a mirror and practice your presentation aloud. Imagine speaking naturally and clearly to your audience.

4. Practice in front of an audience, such as a friend or a parent. Be sure not to hold your report in front of your face.

Now you're ready to present your report to your class!

You can follow the steps in this book every time you are assigned a report. The process will become easier. Soon you will be an expert in both your topic and in report writing!

Glossary

browser	a computer program that allows people to view Web sites
call number	a number on a library book that tells people where to find that book on the shelves
card catalog	an alphabetical listing of the books in a library; it organizes books by subject, title, and author
Dewey Decimal System	a system of numbers that organizes nonfiction books by subject
encyclopedias	books or sets of books that give information on different subjects
entry words	boldface words, usually in alphabetical order, that highlight the subjects or articles on a page in a reference book
guide words	words at the top of a page in a reference book that give the first or last entry on the page
juvenile	having to do with children, such as books written for children
reference books	books with organized information on different subjects, such as encyclopedias and dictionaries
Roman numerals	letters of the Roman alphabet that are used as numbers
search engine	a Web site used to gather information from the Internet

Index

bibliography 21
brainstorming 6
call number 10, 11
card catalog 10, 11
checklist 7
computer 10, 11, 12–13, 20
Dewey Decimal System 10–11
draft 20
editing 20
encyclopedia 3, 8–9
Internet 3, 8, 12–13
keywords 8, 11, 12
note-taking 14–15
outline 16–17, 18
presentation 22
questions 7, 14
revising 20
search engine 12–13
topics, choosing 6–7
Web sites 12–13, 14
work planner 4–5
writing 18–21